COPYRIGHT © 2019. ALL RIGHTS RESERVED.

No part of this publication may be reproduced, distributed, or transmitted in any form or by any means, including photocopying, recording, or other electronic or mechanical methods, or by any information storage and retrieval system without the prior written permission of the publisher, except in the case of very brief quotations embodied in critical reviews and certain other noncommercial uses permitted by copyright law.

Table Of Contents

INTRODUCTION

CHAPTER 1
JESUS TAUGHT THE LAW OF ATTRACTION

CHAPTER 2
USING LAW OF ATTRACTION TO MANIFEST PROSPERITY

CHAPTER 3
LAW OF ATTRACTION AND HOW IT AFFECTS YOUR CHOICES

CHAPTER 4
HOW TO USE THE LAW OF ATTRACTION TO PREVENT FAILURE

CHAPTER 5
HOW TO BENEFIT FROM LAW OF ATTRACTION

CHAPTER 6
THE LAW OF ATTRACTION - THE 7 BIGGEST MYTHS DEBUNKED

CHAPTER 7
HOW USE THE LAW OF ATTRACTION TO GET LASTING WEIGHT LOSS RESULTS

CONCLUSION

INTRODUCTION

WHAT IS IT?

The "Law of Attraction" well you may be asking what is it and what can it do for me? Well first as the name suggests "Law of Attraction" is about attracting the things you want in life and not the things you don't want. Every day, every hour, every minute, every second we are exposed to different things in our lives, it is those things such as the people we talk to, the expensive houses, tangible assets, our bank accounts plus much, much more those are the things we being exposed to everyday.

DID YOU KNOW?

Did you know the most famous, wealthy, entrepreneurs use this application everyday in their lives?

The Law of Attraction is not a complex mathematical formula or anything like that, it is an application that we use every day, how we use it is another story and that is the beauty and the nature of the Law of Attraction. You are either using for you or against you, which in simpler terms is positive push or negative push.

Some people are using the Law of Attraction without them knowing or understanding the nature of it and how if applied correctly with attention to its application can be very beneficial to goal setting, motivation, confidence, creating wealth, exposing your true abilities etc.

Take some of the leaders in business and successful business empires, for example Donald Trump 'A Business Tycoon' now his success is not herald by a miracle or some sort of magic. It is actually herald by what he attracts into his life, what choices he makes, what environment he puts himself, his savvy business ego approach, his planning, his thoughts and his actions. Luck only plays a very small role in some situations and only helps to establish a good outcome, but it is not the basis of Law of Attraction, so don't think, that luck is the basis for these fortunate, famous, wealthy individuals.

Think about this for a moment, if you are always, everyday exposing yourself i.e. hanging around negative, low self-esteem people, did you ever think that this may have an negative impact on your life and well being?

Well that is the environment you put yourself in 'universe' and that is what we mean when we refer to the 'universe' it simply means the surroundings and the environment you put yourself in.

We consequently create our own realities through the use of "The Law of Attraction", regardless if we know we are using it or not. The Law of attraction is working as we speak, for me, for you for everybody; everybody has the power and the ability to use the "Law of Attraction."

POSITIVE THINKING PLAYS AN IMPORTANT ROLE

Positive thinking plays an important role in the Law of Attraction, obviously thinking positively has good outcomes and thinking negative thoughts obviously has the opposite effect. So the obvious choice is to think positive and block out all negativity. When we are able to use the Law of Attraction to our best advantage we can attract the things we want in life, this is part of the positive thinking process, and it is how we perceive those things that we mostly think about and dwell upon.

Those thoughts, thinking, ideas are indeed very powerful, did you know that the mind is the most powerful part of our body metaphorically speaking. Although the theory behind the Law of Attraction sounds relatively simple, putting it into everyday practice requires a little more than what you would expect, yes it takes time and effort. But if applied and practiced correctly it can be very powerful and advantageous to your life on all sorts of levels. It can help you overcome habits and or problems that reside in your life which are giving you a negative impact.

The Law of Attraction has the ability to transform your life into a more buoyant purposeful meaning helping you gain the things you want in your life. The Law of Attraction is not some magical show; The Law of Attraction is an actual science that is recognized amongst many physicists, scientists throughout the world who use the Law of Attraction for the basis for many things.

In fact many people are using the Law of Attraction without realization they are using it, but when you realize the benefits and the steps to achieve greater goals you can no doubt benefit greatly from the Law of Attraction.

THE BASIS OF "THE LAW OF ATTRACTION"

First you must **ask** - You must know what you want to achieve and ask yourself "What is it I really want in life?" The universe can't deliver without first knowing what it is that you want to have manifested into your life, you must be able to ask questions for yourself and answer them with honesty. (The universe is defined as the surroundings the environment you put yourself in)

Believe - You need to truly believe that what you are asking for will become yours. Doubts need to be pushed away. The idea that failure is a possibility will mess up the message.

Receive - It is important that you become an active player in reaching your goals. When opportunity comes your way you must not hesitate.

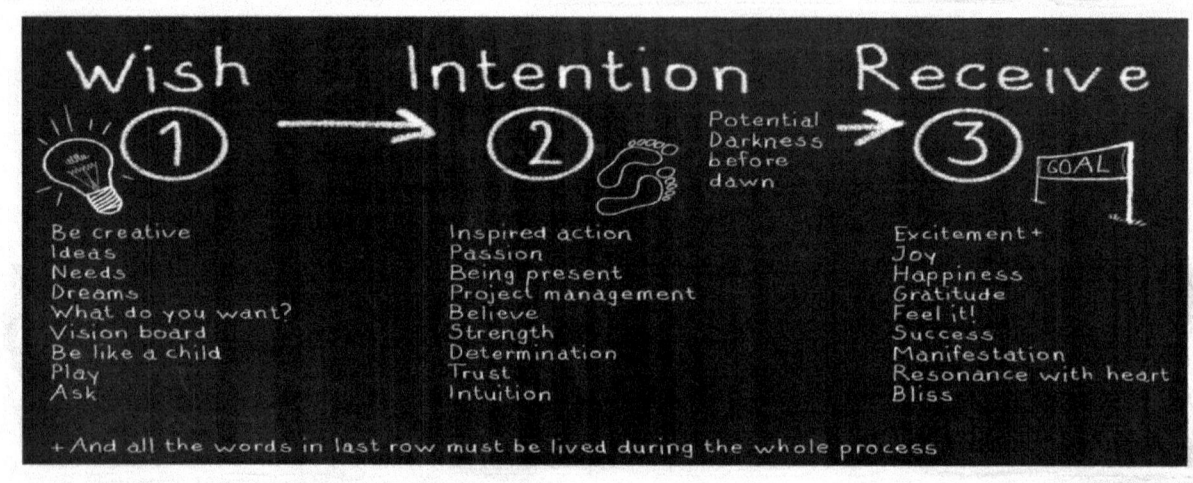

7 Steps to Manifest Anything You Want — Including Money

Step 1: Get clear on what you want.

Step 2: Ask the universe. Ask the universe for what you want once a day makes your requests clearer and clearer.

Step 3: Work toward your goals.

Step 4: Trust the process.

Step 5: Receive and acknowledge what you get.

Step 6: Keep Your Vibration High.

Step 7: Clear your resistance.

> Don't be afraid feeling good now will cancel your 'order' with the Universe because it will think you must not want your 'stuff' anymore.
>
> It doesn't work like that. Feeling good now will just bring you lots of things that match that feeling.

CHAPTER 1

JESUS TAUGHT THE LAW OF ATTRACTION

The Law of Attraction is a popular phenomenon that promotes the theory that you can attract anything you want into your life by thinking about it. Now, this is a 30,000 foot view of the Law of Attraction, because upon closer inspection, there are many other factors that are needed to insure success for manifesting what you want into your life. Religious fundamentalists have criticized the Law of Attraction because of its emphasis on seeking material possessions and because it seems like the Law of Attraction places the power of creation solely upon the individual, as opposed to God, which is not a concept embraced in fundamentalist religious ideology.

The Law of Attraction gained its popularity by the huge success of the book and movie, "The Secret".

If you use only "The Secret" as an argument against the Law of Attraction due to the movie/books simplicity of LOA (Law of Attraction) principles and the hedonistic tone of the movie, I might have to agree. But, the true value of "The Secret" was the mass exposure the book/movie provided to the general public about the concept of LOA. Before the "The Secret" was produced, the idea itself of being a participant in your own life design was totally alien.

There is no doubt that the prevailing attitude of our current culture, whether you're religious or not, is that we are all victims in a tough world, and I thank "The Secret" for opening the door of opportunity to see the world differently.

The initial first look at the principles of the Law of Attraction in "The Secret" was a good introduction, but ironically the true principles of the Law of Attraction have been around for over 2000 years, in fact, they were taught to us by Jesus. The Law of Attraction, when studied deeply and from a metaphysical level, is really an opportunity to live our lives the way that Jesus taught us to do, infinitely and abundantly.

Matthew 6:33

"But seek ye first the kingdom of God, and his righteousness; and all these things shall be added unto you."

At first glance, Jesus words above might imply that we have a huge task to fulfill before we can get to the good part for us, (things added unto you). But perhaps the above words from Jesus holds more to it than we thought possible before.

Many traditional religions teach that life is successful, happy, fulfilling, etc., or not, by the manner in which we conduct ourselves according to the religious rules/principles, and by doing so, we create a positive or negative flow into our lives. (seek the Kingdom of God first THEN the you will be rewarded accordingly). Yet, a devoutly religious person may do everything their religion says they should do, and yet still experience great hardships and suffering in their lives. This is sometimes attributed to being the will of God or part of a plan that God has for you. Or, these hardships may be because you clearly have not been "seeking the Kingdom of God first". While there may be some spiritual sanction in the text for these traditional religious beliefs, the precept that you are not a participant in your own life design, other than to live by the rules mandated in order to receive your blessings in this life or the next, is highly subjective and clearly interpretive. Religious themes leave out the fact that as a child and image of God, that you, yourself, have amazing power as well.

The find God principle taught in almost all religious belief systems, is what I call the top down approach to spiritual connection. God is above and we are below and it is our responsibility to reach out to God by following these rules and opening our hearts and then all should be pretty good for us in the here and here after. In the approach, we start with a baseline of separateness and use religion and ideology as a way to connect to God. In other words, we don't go to church to learn about our power because of our inseparable relationship with God, instead we learn what God has done for us already, separately from us, to encourage us to connect to a relationship with God.

The notion of learning about God, and I mean connecting to God in a seriously intimate and powerful way, comes by first looking within ourselves and therein finding God. This is what I call the bottom up approach to connecting to God. In this approach, our baseline starts with us being ALREADY connected and using our own divine power within to discover and awaken to God and the Divine Universe, which includes the LOA principles. It is in this approach to spiritual connection and personal empowerment that true LOA processes begin.

So another interpretation of our earlier Bible verse that may more closely align with our innate power and divine inheritance is:

"But seek (discover, obtain) ye first the kingdom of God, (the divine power of God manifested in you) and his righteousness; (God's qualities, such as worth, value, abundance, and joy that is already within you), and all these things (human and spiritual wants and needs related to what you find within you) shall be added unto you." (Matthew 6:33)

And to support the kingdom of God verbiage (because without the following words from Jesus, the kingdom of God could be construed to be some faraway or unknown place), Jesus clarifies for us where the kingdom of God is located.

Luke 17:21

"Neither shall they say, Lo here! or, lo there! for, behold, the kingdom of God is within you."

The Law of Attraction also teaches that in order to manifest the things that we want to see realized into our lives, we must go within as well. The greatest LOA teachers will equate the powerful visualization and certainty of our strongest desires to a heartfelt calling from your inner divine being. Manifesting a new trinket for pure pleasure may be possible by the power of a strong energetic will, but this parlor trick is not a true Law of Attraction principle. LOA principles operate from a fundamental certainty that God and man, cooperatively manifest from the infinite possibilities available within each one of us (kingdom of God within).

The exact Law of Attraction definition simply states that "like attracts like", which is another way of saying that we live within our true beliefs. So, the best start for a successful LOA practice is to think and act from our existing beliefs (go within). Certainly it is possible with a strong belief, and an undeniable firm conviction, to manifest just about anything. But for those only looking for a new distractions and material possessions to manifest for the purposes of status, ego gratification, or neediness, then you have missed the true power of the Law of Attraction.

You may be able to apply LOA principles to get what you want, but then next day, the want will still be there. The bottom line is you can think and attract all you want, but the core element of practicing a successful and powerfully beneficial Law of Attraction practice is first starting within to manifest from a divine and authentic belief system. Know where your power comes from, which is from the kingdom of God within you. Applying the LOA principles from a position of divine strength, by going within, to see the enfoldment of all the "things" that will be added unto you (via our beliefs), is the Law of Attraction being practiced as Jesus taught.

Now, the next steps in a successful Law of Attraction practice were also taught by Jesus in many different examples in the Bible. We will address the next fundamental step of LOA principles, which is your belief in the power of manifestation and what you are manifesting, in Part 2 of this article. For this article, the main concept to consider is this: The Law of Attraction is a process of living a life of unlimited potential within your own divine authority (kingdom of God within). We all have the ability to do this, but the reasons we are unsuccessful at it are: we ask and desire from an inauthentic mindset (our desires do not match a true need that wants to be met), we don't really believe in the process or in the thing that we are asking for, and we do not "live" within the divine authority to create the life we want. All of these problems with the LOA process will be addressed in the next segment and additional teachings of Jesus will be referenced to demonstrate how Jesus also taught the Law of Attraction.

Law of Attraction - **Like Attract Like**

Step One - Before you go manifesting things like, days off from work, cars, money, or for your ex-husband to get the crabs, you MUST identify what you really want and where the want comes from. Want that comes from neediness, resentment, revenge, unworthiness, fear, and lack, are inauthentic wants (meaning they come from the ego and not from the divine higher self), and you may succeed in manifesting some of your wants but they will never satisfy the authentic need.

This does not mean you cannot manifest material "things", it just means that your manifestation must come from "within" to be a true Law of Attraction principle in action. This is why Jesus instructs us to find the kingdom of God (within) before the things are added to us. Know where your power comes from and understand what your true wants are.

Proverbs 29:18,
Where there is no vision, the people perish.

JESUS CHRIST REVEALED THE SECRET LAW OF ATTRACTION

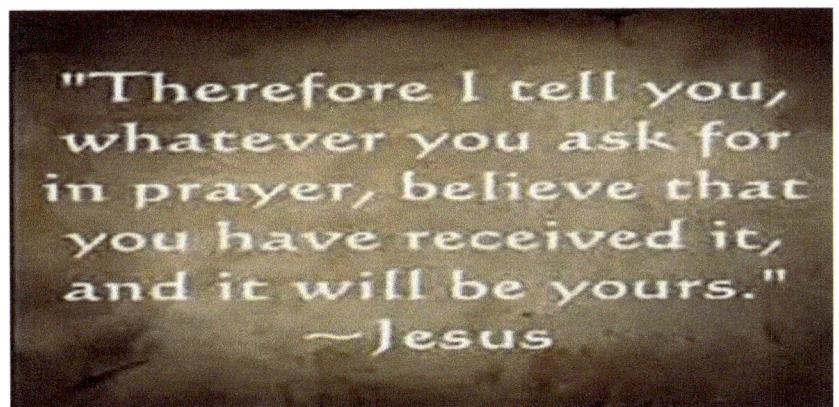

CHAPTER 2

USING LAW OF ATTRACTION TO MANIFEST PROSPERITY

Nothing is, unless your thinking makes it so. -Shakespeare

Do you use the law of attraction effectively to manifest your dreams? If you've already watched the movie 'The secret' and all those exceptionally successful people who appear to effortlessly attract what they want, you might be "thinking": there's definitely more to it than just thinking. You guessed it... There is!

World renowned author and coach, Bob Proctor believes there are 11 forgotten laws in the Universe, which includes the law of attraction.

Surely you can't just sit there and visualize what you want and then turn into a magnet and watch it come into your life like magic. So how do many people find the law of attraction so effective in manifesting what they long for? They grasped the various ways of using the law of attraction in combination with the other laws of the Universe.

The Connecting Link

In the Old Testament it was written:

Proverbs 23:7

As a man thinketh in his heart, so is he.

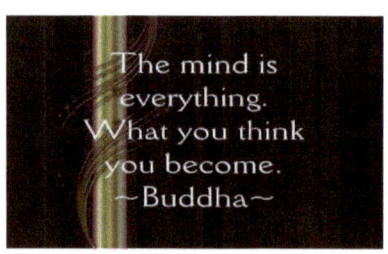

This is how the law of attraction works, through thoughts that manifest into things, but this does not necessarily mean that thoughts of your desires will just turn into what that you desire. Rather thoughts become ideas, and beliefs become convictions that cause you to act and those actions become results.

And what kinds of results are we talking about? Everything in the Universe vibrates including our thoughts. Therefore the results we are talking about must be consistent with the vibration of our thoughts, which become beliefs that become convictions, which we turn into actions, which turn into results.

Therefore, your thoughts are the "seeds" which you plant, and as those grains are nourished and tended in a while, they begin to propagate until these deliberate thoughts become actions. And as you know, a seed cannot produce something which is inconsistent with its intrinsic design. As the Nazarene said: "You will know them by their fruit...you can't get grapes from thorn bushes and you can't get figs from thistles."

So your predominant thoughts will eventually be expressed in the results you get in your life. The reason people sometimes think it doesn't work is because they work with man-made time which is inconsistent with getting the law of attraction to work for you...

What Season are You In?

When you got up to make your breakfast this morning, you probably slapped something into the microwave, pushed a few buttons and within a few minutes had a nice hot meal. But this is not how the law of attraction works when it comes to realizing the results you want. You see, the law of attraction is a natural law, not artificially made. And so it is governed by the same principles that direct other laws of the universe. Nothing will change this. It's an unchangeable reality of the universe which established the law of attraction. Remember, the thoughts that you "plant"

when you're using the law of attraction bring forth results the same way that a grain you plant in the ground germinates into a tree. Long before the seed sprouts, you have to first sow the grain, water and tend to it.

This also means no normal persons digs up the seed and sows something else every few hours or days. You have to decide what you desire, plant the seed and tend to it long enough for the law of attraction to do its job.

For most of us, the hardest thing to do is to decide what we want and to have an unshakable belief even when the result is not instant. Bear in mind, everything starts with your thoughts... so for a while, that's all you have.

Persevere even if your actions are seemed inconsistent with your thoughts. Remain focused and listen to your inner voice and be patient and consistent, you will reap a great harvest in time... if you persevere.

CHAPTER 3

LAW OF ATTRACTION AND HOW IT AFFECTS YOUR CHOICES

The Law Of Attraction like all Universal Law is dependably at work and dependably conveys correctly what YOU choose.

All things that exist inside our universe are made out of vitality, or vibration. The Law of Attraction keeps it streaming easily and flawlessly.

What is this perplexing and "apparently elusive" Law called The Law of Attraction?

Well. honestly its not as secretive, "apparently exclusive" or hard to see as such a large number of "see" it to believe it. It's just a question of getting to be mindful of it and figuring out how to deliberately orchestrate with it to start encountering a kind and personal satisfaction that many people "unwittingly pick" NOT to experience.

Truth be told its so straight forward, once you have an essential understanding of it and are given a chance to perceive and see for yourself exactly how basic it truly is, you'll completely see how to make it function for you through deliberately centered proposition and with a consistency that more than likely will "shock" you.

That is the thing that we'll be investigating here. We'll be giving you a completely clear understanding of both what The Law of Attraction is, the manner by which and why it lives up to expectations the way it does and above all how YOU can make it work for you... consciously, purposefully and reliably in every single part of your life.

The Law of Attraction, otherwise called and referred to as Circumstances and end results or Sowing and

Procuring is, similar to all Widespread Laws, amazingly essential to comprehend and deliberately execute on the off chance that you are to figure out how to intentionally and deliberately draw in the longings of your heart into your life. Just as imperative is to figure out how not to draw in those things that you don't fancy.

The Law of Attraction Is Unchanging and Immovable.

The Law of Attraction, in the same way as all other All inclusive Laws, can't be changed, gotten away from or controlled by anybody. Much the same as the Law of Gravity, the Law of Attraction is continually at work and never rests. These laws alluded to as general laws, regular laws, or laws of nature have existed since the start of time itself and will stay into forever. They are not subject to alteration by you or I.

Much the same as the majority of the other All inclusive Laws, the Law of Attraction will keep on operating efficiently, perfectly, and with 100% enduring assurance paying little respect to your consciousness of it or lack of awareness to it. It will keep on operating precisely as it was made, paying little heed to your conviction or unbelief in it.

The Law of Attraction conveys to all, in precisely the same system, and with the same faithful and unsurprising assurance, paying little mind to your age, sex, religious conviction, nationality, and so on. It doesn't separate, segregate or judge in any capacity, shape or structure. You can't escape it or departure its belongings.

The main control that you, as an individual have over it, is to "deliberately" practice your decision or through and through freedom, concerning what you offer (vibration) to it to work with. That giving of yourself to it, figures out what you should get in exchange.

In the event that you decide to intentionally make a certain result, you should first figure out how to deliberately adjust your contemplations, convictions and feelings with the sought conclusion which will without come up short and with 100% relentless sureness permit you to draw in whatever is wanted. By the same token, in the event that you provide for it, or resound considerations and feelings of alarm, tension, need, impediment, and so on., you can just and will draw in business as usual.

For those that decide to intentionally make and carry on with a life of plenitude and satisfaction, this is Extraordinary News!

Why?

Since by getting to be mindful and creating an understanding of how the Law of Attraction works and deliberately adjusting your musings and feelings with its undeniable, unflinching and unsurprising operation, you can then utilize (actualize) it, to pull in to yourself, particular outcomes... desired conclusions that before obtaining this information, appeared to happen just by a long shot.

However first and foremost, on the off chance that you are to use its energy to start to intentionally make what you seek, you should first have a consciousness of its operation.

That is the thing that you are going to find here... how to deliberately, purposefully, intentionally and reliably use the Law of Attraction for start pulling in to yourself the wanted conclusions in EVERY aspects of your life physically, fiscally, socially, candidly and/or profoundly.

It will then turn into your decision whether to acknowledge or deny it as truth in spite of the fact that the refusal to acknowledge and recognize it won't change the way that it is because of The Law of Attraction's unfaltering and unsurprising nature that you are encountering the life comes about that you have, right now are and dependably will.

Actually, your mindfulness or unawareness of its presence has truly no impact on its operation any more than your consciousness of or confidence in gravity would have ZERO impact on its steady and permanent operation.

We should dig into and investigate how and why that is "true"...

As clarified in the Law Of Vibration and Quantum Physics articles. Everything that a person can physically involved with the five human faculties of sight, hearing, taste, touch, and smell, softened down and dissected up there most essential sub-nuclear structure, comprises of subatomic structures known as subatomic particles additionally alluded to as vitality or vibration. In the same way, the unseen things that can't be sensed with the five essential human faculties, for example, your contemplations, feelings, oxygen, and so on are likewise, when broken down into their most fundamental structure and dissected, vibration or vitality.

So how would you give that information something to do for you, utilizing the Law of Attraction?

In the first place, we should recap what we've officially learned.

1) All things (seen and unseen) softened down and dissected up there purest and most fundamental structure, comprise of vitality or vibrations.

2) Considerations are a vibration

3) Our reality and everything inside it, first started with a thought.

4) The considerations that we think (seeds) are just emitted vibrational frequencies which are show into the Universe drawing in to them vibrations of the same vibrational reverberation or recurrence which makes (shows) what we come to see and involvement in our physical world as our current reality. (Our Life)

Exploratory take a look at The Law of Attraction

Above all else how about we investigate what established researchers says in regards to the Law of Attraction.

It Expresses: The Law of Attraction is the law by which thought associates with its protest.

We should take a look at this in a more physical sense, using physically perceptible material that we can see and are mindful of once a day, to fulfill the logical left cerebrum and visual sort of individuals.

The accompanying analysis will permit you to see the Law of Attraction in activity from a physical viewpoint.

A straight forward Analysis To Accept The Law of Vibration

As a matter of first importance we'll take two eye droppers, and fill unified with oil and the other with water. Next, drop one drop of water onto a surface. Presently take the other (oil) and spot a drop on top of the drop of water. What happens? Do they join together and get to be as one, or does one repulse the other? Clearly they repulse one another. However why is this? They are both a fluid substance and it appears they ought to meet up into one mass.

The reason is as basic as the Law of Attraction.

Both substances are of a fluid birthplace, each one have their own particular individual subatomic cosmetics which is not the same as the other (varying subatomic structures which resound and venture an alternate vibration or vitality recurrence)

Without getting into the definite experimental recipes and subatomic structures, that make up every substance and the numerical mathematical statements that help this, in there most fundamental structure, such as everything in our reality, they comprise of vibration or vitality.

The vitality or vibration that is emitted from each is diverse due to the changing structures of particles and sub-nuclear particles that each one contains which make them vibrate or resound at distinctive frequencies. Since they vibrate at diverse frequencies they are not able to be pulled in to one another and therefore really repulse the other.

Alright, how about we proceed with our trial. In the event that you were to utilize the same process as above, aside from this time, drop a solitary drop of water and afterward put an alternate drop of water specifically on top in the first place, what happens? The two join together as one, in light of the fact that the subatomic cosmetics or structure, or rate of vibration, (vitality) of the two is precisely the same. This brings us to the conclusion that like vibrations or frequencies of vitality that "orchestrate" with different frequencies pulls in to itself like vibrations.

So it is with the Law of Attraction. Whatever thought vitality (vibrating seed) that you discharge into the universe, makes and emanates a particular vibratory example or recurrence focused around the kind and nature of thought, is pulled in by and joined with like vitality of the same symphonious recurrence or vibration which vibrates in reverberation with it, which thus make the occasions, conditions and circumstances that you see show in your life each and every day!

You are actually pulling in to yourself, the thing thought of (harvest).

There is a staggering measure of late experimental proof accessible that backings the truths of the Law of Attraction, and incorporates the greater part of the mathematical statements, tests, and so on that undeniably demonstrate reality behind this wonder. By all means... please don't take my word or any other individual words.

Do your research and make your own decision (see [Quantum Material science](#)). For the purpose of those that get it as of right now, how about we move to the other worldly angles that backing the presence and immovable operation of The Law of Attraction which for some will support in accepting its "truth.

THE LAW OF VIBRATION:

Everything from thought to radiant energy from the sun runs at a frequency and through out life we are constantly tuning this frequency to different radio channels to get information to survive.

CHAPTER 4

HOW TO USE THE LAW OF ATTRACTION TO PREVENT FAILURE

When you decide to do something, one thing comes up immediately. It is the expectation of the result from your actions. There are only two alternatives here. It is either you get the result you want or you fail to get it. The law of attraction has been known for years for being one of the secrets to success in life. This section is about how to use law of attraction to prevent failure in your life.

The Law of attraction states that you can attract good things into your life by your good thinking. It can be other way around with bad things and bad thinking.

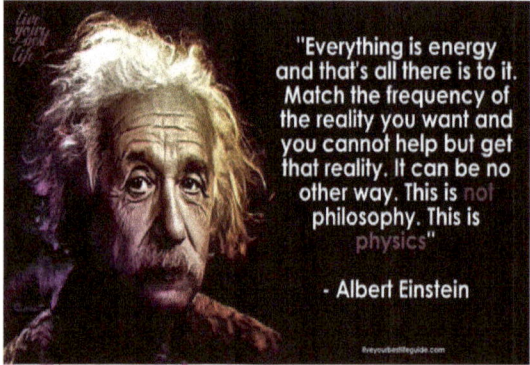

To make use of the law of attraction is to think correctly. The following steps are to train your mind to think systematically. This is one of the ways to use the law of attraction. Then we go into the actions of planning and implementing. We then exercise the law by visualization. The steps to prevent failure include:

1. **Change the definition of failure.**

Before I go further on how to prevent failure, we should first go to the definition of failure. Longman dictionary gives to definitions of failure as the lack of Success, things that fail, non-performance or non-production of something, inability of a business to continue.

These definitions are somehow easy to understand as standard definition. This is why most people are afraid of failure. Failure is viewed as intimidated force to destroy our confidence. A lot of people have so much fear of failure that they dare not to set up their goals or try anything new. We need to change that. We need to understand that success and failure come together. All successful people understand this. They do not fear failure. Failure is the stepping stones to success. You can have many stepping stones. You need to treat failure as one of the element to succeed. Every time you meet failure, just tell yourself that you are one step closer to your success.

2. **Determine that you are going to succeed.**

Having the right mindset on your determination is another key factor. You need to decide that you want the result no matter what. You have to determine the price you need to pay before you make the decision. Once you are sure, go for it. You need to go all the way until you succeed. In order to be able to do that, you need to have a firm commitment to yourself. You need to determine that you are going to succeed and you are ready to do what it takes.

3. **Be clear on your goals.**

You need to know exactly what you want in your actions. What are your goals and why you want them? What are the benefits of achieving your goals? What will happen if you don't achieve them? All these questions need to be answered before you start. Most people are not clear on what they want because they have not made the decision. This is why the majority of the people in the society do not succeed in fully utilizing their capacity. You don't have to be one of them. Once you are clear on your goal, you can proceed without any equivocal hesitation on your mind.

4. **Set up your plan. Break down your plan into small plan.**

You need to have the action plan in your steps. Make the big picture plan and break it down into small plans. The small plans are for seeing your progress and you can celebrate when you achieve these small goals. Planning is essential to your action so do not neglect it.

5. **Take action and evaluate them along the way.**

You can not succeed without doing something. You need to take action. You need to take more of the right actions in order to enjoy more fruitful results. In addition, you need to evaluate yourself along the way. You need to see if there is anything to be improved. Is your current approach correct? Are you on the right track? All these evaluations will help you to align your actions until you get to your goals.

6.**Visualize your way to succeed.**

Visualization is the most effective way to use the law of attraction. It will stimulate your subconscious mind. The mind will attract all circumstances and attributes favorable to what you visualized. You can do it by visualizing that you are getting what you want as if it is happening in front of you. You can feel it and have that feeling penetrate into your mind. You can use background audio to enhance your visualization power. There are many in the market and Attraction Accelerator can be one of your choices.

The law of attraction can be used to prevent the failure to happen in your life. This book talks about the steps to fully utilize the law.

CHAPTER 5

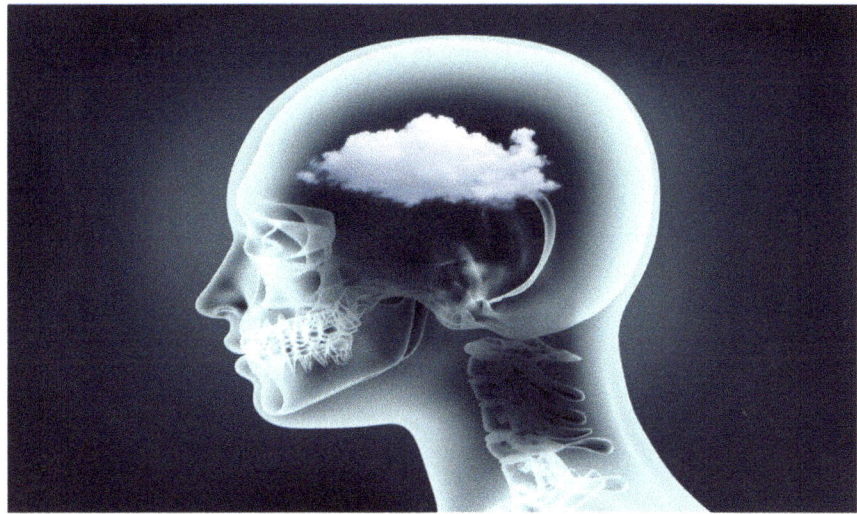

HOW TO BENEFIT FROM LAW OF ATTRACTION

Almost everyone is well aware of "The Secret", the theory that brings theories like law of attraction and positive thinking to normal conversations. Although The Secret has been a recent phenomenon, according to the spiritual thinkers they have been studying this concept for many years. The acclaimed author of The Secret Rhonda Byrne is known to be the mother of this concept that is Positive Thinking.

Everyone uses the law of attraction in their daily lives but very few of them realize it, so they miss the chance of deliberately creating what they desire. Since the release of this new topic there have been many discussions about it and everyone is trying to know how to achieve it.

Some people have practiced it hard and now have been successful enough to create real law of attraction success stories in their lives. Although there are many sayings and many teachings regarding it, the basic concept is same in all of them.

Relax your mind.

Relax and meditate for few minutes. This will help in increasing your brain power, relaxing, and focusing your mind. Although this step is optional you really should always do it.

Be sure about what is needed and never doubt

You will be sending your request to the universe and other supreme powers so be sure about what you are asking for. If you yourself will be unclear then the giving power will also be not sure what to give. Once decided never doubt if you will get it or not. So have great enthusiasm and always be sure about what you want without doubting yourself.

Dedication and sincerity.

Ask the universe for what you want with complete faith and dedication. Never let any negative thought come in your mind for any length of time.

What you think is what you will get.

You cannot be both positive and negative at the same time.

If you think positively then the same will get attracted and if you think negative then the negative things will get attracted. It is plain and simple.

Show gratitude.

Always be grateful towards the universe. Be content in what you have and be thankful for what you will be getting in future. Be thankful to the universe for giving you life and fulfilling your wishes. Showing gratitude will in a way boost the energy of the universe and will help you in receiving more. But be sincere after all it is the one that is the main source of everything and much superior to us.

Have Faith.

Think of a dimension that is running in parallel to our world where all wishes come true and you are in that place. Imagine yourself there and ask whatever you want from the universe and see your wishes getting fulfilled in an instant. Other than that, never focus on what you are asking. The tricky part comes here and most people mess up this part.

If you focus on your wish then it will be like telling the universe that you don't have it, and the universe will obey you and won't give you that thing. This is called negative thinking. Instead of focusing on you don't have, focuses on the idea that you have it and you will get it now. This is called positive thinking.

Just have faith and believe that you will have it and definitely universe will fulfill all your wishes.

Think only what you want.

Most people think of what they don't want all the time. They focus on how miserable their life is instead of how to get what they want. They blame other people or situation for their own failure. This is a normal way of human behavior. It is a defense mechanism that came with us since we were born. Human wants to be right. Our instinct makes it that way. The good news is that we can control our thoughts. And so we can control our future. Make a decision now to focus only on what you want so that you can attract the favorable situation for your goal achievement.

Plan your day and take actions toward your goal.

Although Law of Attraction helps us on attracting the situation we want, we need to also do our part. It doesn't mean that we don't have to do anything. We will not benefit from the situation if we don't do what we are supposed to do. We have to have our goals set. We need to write down our plan and take actions toward our goals. There is no exception to anybody. We need to take massive actions to get success. There is no other way.

Visualize Regularly.

One of the most powerful ways to use the law of attraction is to make visualization. Regular visualization will send the right signal to the subconscious mind. The subconscious mind will work on the attraction from our visualization. Visualize the situation you want and feel as if it is happening in front of you right now. If you make visualization regularly and effectively, it will attract those images into reality. You may want to add background audio to accelerate your attraction. There are many in the market. Attraction Accelerator can also be one of your choices.

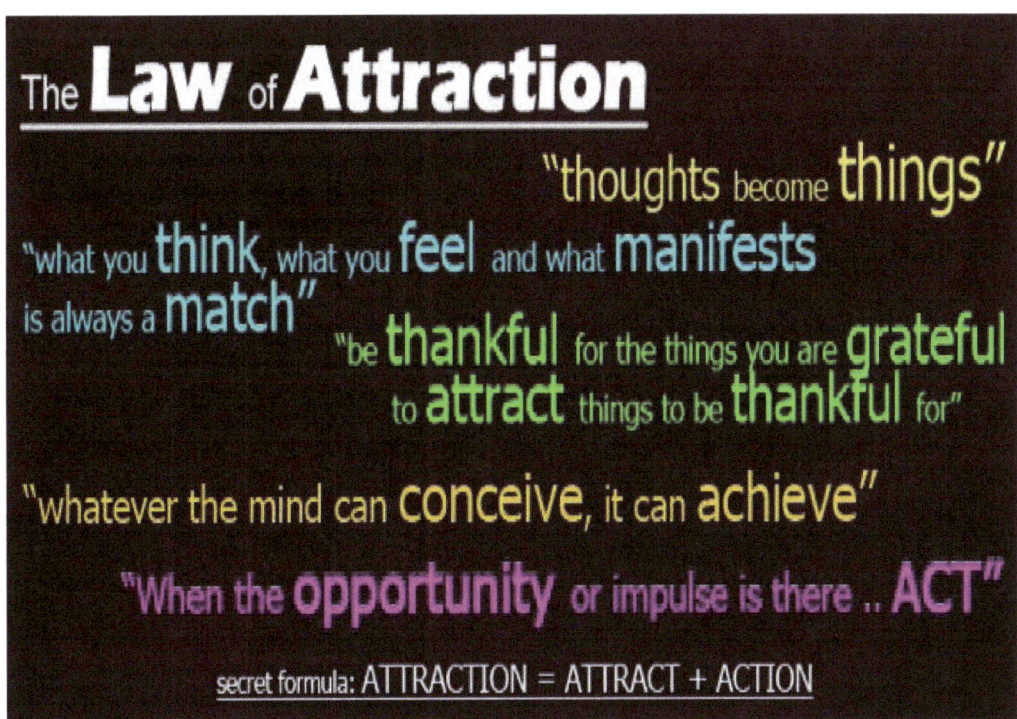

CHAPTER 6

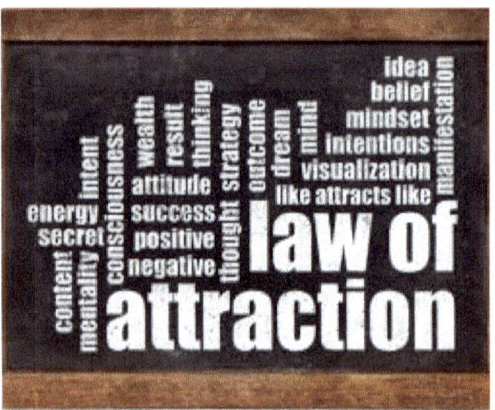

THE LAW OF ATTRACTION - THE 7 BIGGEST MYTHS DEBUNKED

The Law of Attraction has received a great deal of media attention in recent years. Thanks to the movie The Secret and the subsequent explosion of television, print media and internet coverage, nearly everyone in Western society has heard the phrase "Law of Attraction". Most people, however, have picked up snippets and incomplete information here and there and don't really have a solid understanding of how the law works.

This has led to a wide spread misunderstanding of how the Law of Attraction really works, or whether or not it even works at all. A lot of people feel a deep resonance when they are told that they create their own reality. They recognize a truth in this idea. However, they often quickly become frustrated when they're exposed to incomplete information and myths, and can't seem to make it work. They "know" that there's something to this, they can feel it; but they just don't know how to use it yet.

This book aims to debunk the seven biggest myths currently circulating about the Law of Attraction and bring some clarity to the subject.

Myth #1: The Law of Attraction is magic

The Myth: "Law of Attraction advocates will tell you that all you have to do is think positively and the stuff you want will just come to you. Obviously this is wrong, since things like money, cars and houses don't just appear out of thin air."

The Myth Debunked: No one with a true understanding of the Law of Attraction has ever claimed that if you just think a positive thought, a house with a million dollars on the kitchen table and a Ferrari in the driveway will just drop out of the sky right in front of you. This is usually a quote used by people trying to claim that the Law of Attraction is a scam. But the quote isn't true. That isn't how the Law of Attraction works at all.

The Law of Attraction doesn't just literally drop stuff in your lap. It brings you meetings with just the right people at the right time, brilliant ideas and coincidences. It's your job to pay attention to those ideas, follow your hunches and recognize the coincidences.

For example, you'd like to manifest a house. The Law of Attraction gives you an insight to drive through a certain neighborhood that you don't normally drive through. You see a house with a For Sale sign in the yard. The house looks perfect, except you're pretty sure it's completely out of your price range. You decide to stop and knock on the door anyway. It turns out the owners are a lovely couple who are moving to Australia in a month. You and owners really hit it off and they decide to offer you terms that you can afford. They really want you to live there. So, you get the perfect house at a price you're able to pay, under circumstances that you never could've predicted. Did it drop right into your lap? Well, not literally, no. But if you paid attention and followed the insights and impulses the Universe was delivering to you, it could've seemed almost as easy as if it had. This is how the Law of Attraction brings you things. It finds whatever you're looking for that is also looking for you and brings you together through a series of perfect events, insights and hunches.

Myth #2 - All you have to do is visualize

The Myth: "The Law of Attraction is just about visualization. That's why they tell you to create vision boards and the like. You're supposed to stare at the things you want and they will just come to you.

The Myth Debunked: This one is partially true. Visualization can be a valuable tool you use to train yourself to create what you want. It isn't the visualization that creates, though. You create through the vibration that you offer. The vibration you offer is determined by the thoughts you habitually think (beliefs). Visualization can help you to retrain your thoughts, but there's much more to it than that. If you visualize a beautiful car, but have the belief that you'll never get a car like that, you can visualize all day, every day, and that car's not going to show up. How do you know if you harbor a conflicting belief? You can tell by the way you feel when you visualize. If it feels really, really good to visualize the car, and the entire visualization is positive, you're doing well. If, however, it feels a bit off and your visualization takes a bit of a negative turn, you've just uncovered some negative beliefs.

For example, you wonder how you'll afford the payments, which would point to a belief that states "I can't afford a new car"; or you might hope your kids don't mess up the beautiful new seats, which could point to a belief that you can't have nice things and they always get ruined, so, why bother anyway...

Visualization is a valuable tool in manifestation, but it isn't the creation process itself.

Myth #3 - The Law of Attraction is new

The Myth: "If the Law of Attraction is really a law, why hasn't anyone discovered it before? This is just some new fad."

The Myth Debunked: The Law of Attraction isn't new. It's been around since the beginning of time. It can be argued that it's the oldest law in the Universe. The reason that so many people are hearing about it now, is because more and more people are waking up and realizing, or at least getting a glimpse of, who they really are. More people are asking for this information than ever before, and therefore, the Law of Attraction must bring them more answers than ever before. There are more books written on this subject than we've ever seen. Thanks to the internet, people can find answers to their questions immediately.

The information is not "new"; we are simply asking for and able to receive more information, and at a faster rate than ever before. Also, we are living in a time where most of us can discuss spiritual matters and Universal laws openly without fear of being burned at the stake or stoned to death. All of this has allowed the idea of the Law of Attraction to spread at an unprecedented rate.

Myth #4 - The Law of Attraction is Non-Christian

The Myth: "I am a Christian and therefore I cannot believe in the Law of Attraction. This is just a bunch of stuff that conflicts with Christian beliefs"

The Myth Debunked: This one could not be further from the truth. There are hundreds of passages in the Bible that refer to the Law of Attraction. Some of these verses can be traced back almost 3000 years. Jesus said "Everything is possible to him who believes." And "He that believeth on me, the works that I do shall he do also; and greater works than these shall he do..." Here are few more: "As a man thinketh, so he is." (Proverbs 23:7). "It is through thinking that man forms that which he has in life". (Proverbs 23:7). "For everyone who asks receives; he who seeks finds; and to him who knocks, the door will be opened." (Matthew 7:8)

These, and many other scripters just like them, support the principle that your thoughts create your reality and you can create anything you want. The point is that Christianity and the Law of Attraction are not based on inherently conflicting principles. There are actual internet sites on the web dedicated to the study of the Law of Attraction from a Christian point of view.

Myth #5 - I have to do something to make the Law of Attraction "work"

The Myth: "You have to know how to use the Law of Attraction in order to get it to work. If it isn't working for you, you must be doing it wrong."

The Myth Debunked: This is another myth that is based on a complete misunderstanding of how the Law of Attraction works. There is nothing you have to do, or in fact can do to make the Law of Attraction work. Just as there is nothing you have to do or can do to make gravity work. It just works. That's why it's called a law.

You create your own reality. You can't help it. You're a lean, mean, creating machine. Everything you see around you, every person in your life, everything in your reality, is there in response to the vibration you offer. There's nothing you have to do to make that process work, nor can you stop it. That's why no one can claim that "it isn't working for them.

The problem arises when people are creating by default, which often brings them things they don't really want, instead of creating deliberately. Your job is to remember how powerful you really are. That's it. It's not supposed to be hard work. It's supposed to be fun. If you're not having fun, you're doing it wrong.

Myth #6 - Thoughts are dangerous. You have to control every thought you think.

The Myth: "You have to control every thought you think. If you think a 'negative' thought, or have a fear of something, you automatically create that. So watch every thought you think!"

The Myth Debunked: While it's true that every thought has the power to create, there are two big reasons why you don't have to be afraid of your thoughts.

First, one little thought doesn't have all that much power. The power comes from thinking the same thought over and over again, until it's a belief. The more you think a thought and believe it, the more it affects your vibration and it's this vibration that attracts your manifestations. The Law of Attraction responds to your vibration, not the words you've said or thought (although notice that your words and thoughts can affect your vibration).

Second, we have this amazing thing called time. There is a time buffer between offering a vibration and receiving a manifestation. And while many of us often curse this time buffer in our impatience to receive the things we want, it is incredibly useful. Things don't happen immediately for a reason. You have time to notice if you're harboring any conflicting beliefs or are offering a vibration that doesn't really serve you.

For example, if you're driving down the street and have a random thought "I hope I don't get in an accident", you might remember reading somewhere that the Universe and your subconscious don't understand negative statements, and you just put "I hope I get in an accident" out there. So, obviously you'd better suck that thought right back in, or else you'll have an accident. Wrong. If you have the thought "I hope I don't get in an accident" but you don't harbor an underlying belief that driving is dangerous and there's a very good chance that you'll get in an accident, your vibration is not going to even begin to match you up with an accident. If your underlying belief is "I'm safe", you'll be safe.

If, however, you do harbor such a belief, formed by many, many thoughts about how you're a victim, how easy it is to get into accidents, how driving is dangerous, reading lots of news stories about how people get in accidents all the time, talking about those stories, etc., that one little thought has just given you an indication that you have an underlying belief. Do you think these thoughts often and easily? Then you might want to do something about that (or buckle up).

The point is, that even though your thoughts help to form your vibration, which creates your reality, it is the vibration behind the thought you have to pay attention to. A random thought that means nothing to you isn't going to create a thing. But a thought that you believe and think over and over again, a thought you give lots of attention to, will affect your vibration and that will create.

Myth #7 - The Law of Attraction just teaches selfishness

The Myth: "The Law of Attraction teaches people to focus on themselves and how they feel, before focusing on others. This is selfish, and that's bad. We have a duty to be selfless."

The Myth Debunked: This myth and the belief that we must be selfless, have caused more burnout among people with great intentions than anything else.

The Law of Attraction does teach selfishness. But selfishness has gotten a really bad rap. There's a huge difference between walking over bodies to get what you want, which is what many people think of when they hear the word "selfish", and not allowing circumstances and other people to dictate your happiness. Giving of yourself with no regard to how you feel until there's nothing left but an empty husk, is neither virtuous nor necessary. The choices are not just between being a self-sacrificing saint or a complete bastard.

The selfishness that the Law of Attraction teaches, is the kind that allows a mother with three little kids to recognize when she's becoming overwhelmed, and give herself permission to take a hot bath and recharge her batteries, without feeling guilty about it. She comes back refreshed and in a better mood. Do you think this will harm or benefit her children? If we take care of ourselves (physically, psychologically AND spiritually), we have so much more to give others. If we focus on our own joy, we can uplift others, and truly help them, instead of commiserating with them in their misery and just supporting them in their being stuck in that vibration.

The more selfish we are, the more joyful we become, the stronger and more unyielding we stand in our vibration of happiness, the more we have to give others, and the more we can give to others without depleting ourselves. True selfishness is the best thing we can do for the world.

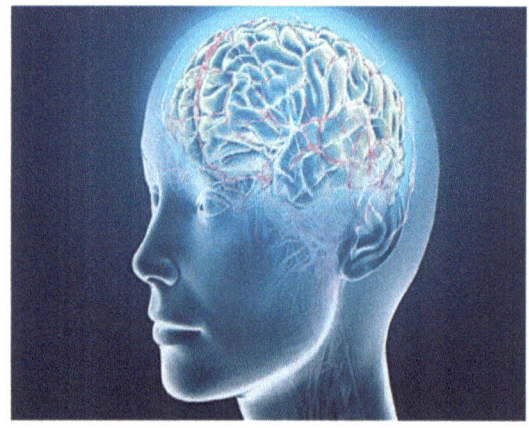

CHAPTER 7

HOW USE THE LAW OF ATTRACTION TO GET LASTING WEIGHT LOSS..

The simple explanation of the law of attraction is that you attract the situations, ideas and positive circumstances in response to the predominant thoughts and desires you hold in your mind. Recently, this phenomenon was explained from a scientific point of view. Your ability to apply the law of attraction to maintain real weight loss results is a fact! In this article I'll help you to understand the key principles of this law and show you how to correctly use it for your weight loss purposes.

The Power of Your Subconscious and Infinite Intelligence

The human brain acts like an outcome-achievement center. Eben Pagan calls our mind "the Google for Goals". Without a doubt, it's one of the most powerful computers on this planet - and we all have free access to it. Our mind consists or two parts: the conscious and the unconscious. The subconscious mind is a neutral and obedient servant of the conscious mind. It acts upon our strong desires and dominant thoughts and beliefs, waiting to implement those commands 24/7. The key distinction here is that the conscious part of our mind may give both positive as well as negative instructions. The sad reality of the situation is that every day our thoughts are more likely to be negative than positive.

This stream of unconstructive message about ourselves creates the program for our subconscious mind, thus manifesting our outer world in accordance with that "software". This can either be good or bad. The way to use this innate mechanism to our benefit is to change the programming of your subconscious mind from negative to positive. The only difficulty is that it can not be done immediately. The negative mental programs creating the circumstances of your life that were formed in the brain during several years cannot be changed easily.

The Most Effective Tool to Change Negative Programming

By now, you're most likely convinced of the fact that our negative beliefs and attitude towards weight loss or any other area can be altered by us. This means we can take control of the results we experience. If you are dieting and exercising, but still not getting big changes in weight reduction, if you see yourself everyday in the mirror and feel frustrated, if you are not confident and not secure, this is how you can change that and attract a fit body by with your thoughts:

Visualize! The visualization is a process of repeated visualization of the fit, healthy, and confident you are aspiring to become. Visualize how you would look when reach your weight loss goals. Think about every detail of your new self...the feeling of confidence and satisfaction that you'll experience. Imagine everything in bright, vivid, and intense colors. Add music to the picture. To supercharge the results of visualization, do the following: make this picture still and mentally throw it up in the air and start making it smaller and smaller until it becomes the size of a small photograph. Then, make it explode into million copies and make it rain...into your future, the present, and past. Don't worry about getting it "right" - your subconscious will help you. Remember, "Thoughts are things", so condition the positive ones and they will help you in your weight loss.

The Magic Behind Written Goals

There is something almost magical about putting what you want onto paper. When you write down what you want in paper every day or at least every other way day, your vision of what it is that you want to achieve becomes clearer, you start believing that you in fact will achieve your goals, and your desire for them magnifies. By writing your goals down in clear, positive, first-person (starting with "I"), and measurable terms -as if by miracle you "transform" and "shift" reality to bring about your desired outcomes. It's also vital to write down all your goals and make specific plans about their accomplishment. Make a plan about what diet you will chose or what changes you will make in your current diet, what you will drink and how you will exercise. It's crucially important to set the dates/deadlines for most of your fitness goals. You have to know where to start and how to measure your results.

How to Talk Your Way Into Weight Loss.

Positive self-talk is a very important technique in the process of weight reduction. Self-talk can be either positive or negative and both of them have big influence on our attitude and behavior. Start to take notice how you are usually talking to yourself and why. You can find out some phrases that closely resemble: I am a lazy..., I will never be slim, I can not stick to healthy diets....

Once you take notice of them, you should begin to use positive and optimistic words and phrases instead even if you might not believe them at first. One powerful way to actively ingrain positive self talk is to set aside 15-20 minutes per day, turn on some music that makes you feel powerful, write down 3 of your goals as positive affirmations, close your eyes, visualize yourself as fit, healthy, confident, and say out loud those affirmations as you clap your hands to the rhythm of the music. While in the shower, on your way home, when you're daydreaming - whenever you can - tell yourself that you look good, that you like yourself, that you will look even better, become more attractive, that you like exercises and that you feel more energetic and committed every day, and that you will persevere and in your weight loss and fitness program.

Action + Repetition = Lifelong Habit

Destructive though patterns and habits cannot be eliminated quickly. As a result, you should repeatedly talk to yourself in a positive way, continue to write down your goals, read encouraging material, and change your focus by thinking about the solutions to your challenges.

Gradually you will form new habits, create a new attitude toward yourself and life and your weight loss challenges will seem like a bad dream you once had. Use the law of attraction everyday, to attract what you want and to form a "I can do attitude!" that will not only bring about a healthy and attractive body, but also decrease the level of stress in your life, and make you a more confident and successful individual.

 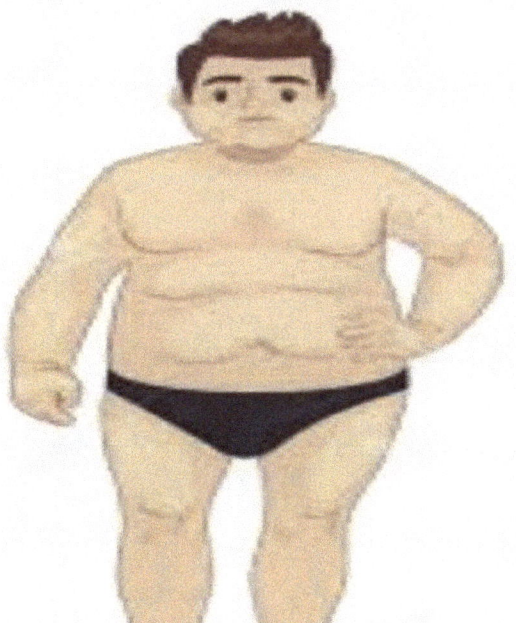

Do not focus on this, which is the problem.

Focus and Visulize, these images of yourself. Which is the solution...

Never Ever Focus on the Problem. Only the

SOLUTION.......

Once you change focus watch your life change

CONCLUSION

The Law of Attraction is among the most ancient universal laws. It just means to depict that whatever circumstances we face in our life are the result of what we thought in our past. Thoughts dominate our mind, they have to manifest in our life. The circumstances we face, the people we meet, the relationships we make, the money we make, the house we live in; these all are the outcome of what we have been thinking with little bit more concentration or simply saying what we have been thinking the most. Have you ever observed when you get angry or frustrated in the morning, it often happens makes your whole day sucks. The "whole day sucks" is a phenomena that is happening because we attracted it in the morning.

What is Law of Attraction?

The law of attraction is a belief or theory, that "like attracts like," and that by focusing on positive or negative thoughts, one can bring about positive or negative results.

Speaking shortly I will define the law of attraction in one line:

"What we think, we manifest"

It's simple. We attract in our daily life with our thoughts and feelings. For example, if we keep thinking that we have no money in our bank account, we will be attracting "no money" in our life. Similarly if we feel like depressed due to workload or other anxieties, we will be welcoming more "depression and anxieties". So we are using this universal law all the time whether we know it or not. Things happening in our daily life are due to this law of attraction.

What Science says?

Thomas Troward, who was among the big guns of the New Thought Movement, claimed that:

"Thought precedes physical form and that "the action of Mind plants that nucleus which, if allowed to grow undisturbed, will eventually attract to itself all the conditions necessary for its manifestation in outward visible form."

Later on metaphysicians also supported the existence of the law of attraction in our daily life. After that the arrival of the book "The Secret" brought up a great revolution in the societies and religious beliefs. So The Law of Attraction is much more the game of your mind set. If you are sincerely able to abide by the principals of the law, you will discover that you can get anything in your life that you love to achieve.

How to Use Law of Attraction:

As I told you earlier that "What we think, we manifest". What we are going to keep in our mind and concentrate on it, we are actually bringing it in the process of manifestation. Using law of attraction is very easy if you keep a firm belief on your thoughts and visualization. Here I will teach you how you can use the law of attraction in your life to get anything you desire to achieve. It consists of only three steps:

1. Ask

2. Feel

3. Give

Ask:

The first step is desire what you want in your life. Definitely you cannot get money if you have not planned to get it. Similarly you will not go for vacation in Spain until you have not planned it. So asking is the first step towards using law of attraction in your life. Sit down, take a pen and paper, relax and think what you desire in your life. Write down everything that comes into your mind whether it's lot of money, a good life partner or whatever... just note it on the paper. Once you have prepared the list of your dreams (wishes), proceed to the next step that is 'feel'.

Feel:

Once you have prepared a list of all of your desires, you have instructed your mind to get ready to achieve. Now start feeling like you have everything in your life that is on that piece of paper (your desires note) and already be grateful for it. If you wrote that you want a lot of money then from now onwards, start feeling like you have lot of money in your account. Bring up that joy in you when you have $100,000 in your account. Feel like you have a perfect partner in your life and you are living a prosperous life. So start imagining that you have access of everything that you have written on that piece of paper and feel gratitude for this abundance. What happens here that the universe begins to listen to your these consistent thoughts and the manifestation process comes into being. So the main theme of this step is:

"What you want to achieve in your life, feel like you already have it"

Give:

The last step in the completion of the law of attraction is "to give". There is a principle in this whole process that states:

"The more you give, the more you get back"

So give from whatever you have in your life. If you can give happiness to someone, go ahead. If you have money, give it without worrying about the amount. Many people get stuck on this step and have some doubts in their minds and they are right at it. As a common person we think that dividing something reduces it. But it is opposite in the law of attraction. This law states that if you give something to someone, you shall get it back multiplied. The question is "How is it possible?" The answer is quite simple and logical. During the give process, you think like you have a lot of something say its money, and you give some money to others. This feeling of abundance ignites the second process that is 'Feel'. So when giving, feel like you already have an abundance of it and you shall have abundance of it. So 'give' process helps in firming your belief that you already have abundance of everything.

This is what law of attraction states.. Ask, feel and give. So the crux of this law lies in your thoughts. Negative thoughts will bring up negative circumstances and vice versa. So start using the law of attraction in your life from now onwards. In the beginning it will take some time to control your thoughts and keep them positive but gradually you will start to have grip over your thoughts and things will start working as the law of attraction will come into action. Its you who can change your life right now and forever. So go ahead and take advantage of this law and be happy. Good luck.

The Law of Attraction is the real deal. It works. But in order to get to the point where you can use it to improve your life, you must first put yourself in the right mindset. A positive attitude is the first step toward implementing the Law of Attraction.

Now that you have a better understanding of the law. You can post how you use the law, in your everyday life, for other to see and share their stories of using the law of attraction. Share your story and everyday life experiences at: www.itsthelaw.info

Get your shirt and apparel at: www.teespring.com/itsthelaw

Follow us on:

Instagram: www.instagram.com/itsthelaw1

Twitter: www.twitter.com/itsthelaw285

Other Books to help you use Law Of Attraction:

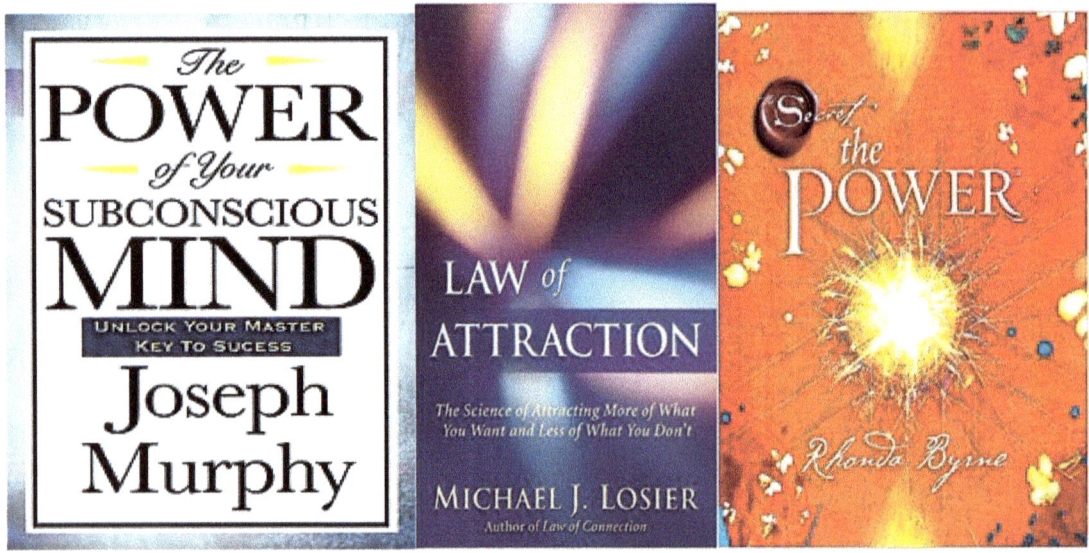

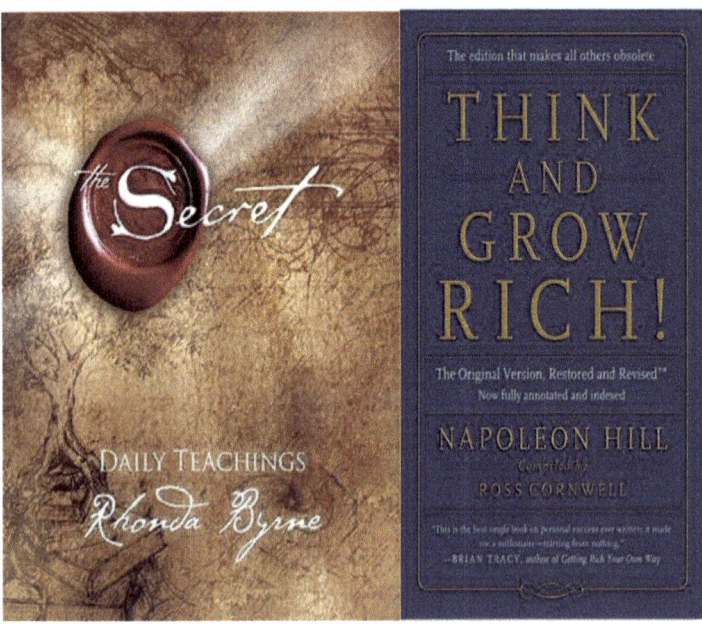

There are many famous people that have died. Such as: Singers, actors, dancers, authors, athletes, rappers etc. If you where ask when where they born or died. Most of us wouldn't know either.

What is known is how great they where at their craft. Their graves have their date of birth and date of death. Now think what's between those two dates? It's a DASH, separating those two dates. It's a small but actually a big symbol of that person's life. We are all living in our DASH right now.

We know our date of birth but don't know when we're going to depart this life. You to can have an effect on peoples life's, by becoming someone who inspires,motivate and help others. Just know how you live your life(Your DASH)now, will determine your legacy. Or how you will be remembered. Make the best of this life(DASH)you've been given and you to can leave something of meaning, that will live long after you have left this life.

Do not go yet; One last thing to do

If you enjoyed this book or found it useful I'd be very grateful if you'd post a short review on Amazon. Your support really does make a difference and I read all the reviews personally so I can get your feedback and make this book even better.

Thanks again for your support!

www.ingramcontent.com/pod-product-compliance
Lightning Source LLC
Chambersburg PA
CBHW061147010526
44118CB00026B/2900